T0042975

"If song takes up where talk breaks down, Derrick Harriell's *Come Kingdom* sings what families refuse. These poems cast wisdom in riddles, twenty-first century syncopated blues. Physics says a voice echoes back in reverse. Harriell's poems show life bounce between generations, voice gather flesh in refraction. *Come Kingdom* goes from here to the broken, gone to the chronic, the subtractive to happenstatic. The rule seems to be this: Every kingdom's mostly what it isn't, so it's on us. Come with it." —ED PAVLIĆ

"What a book. It hurts, it redeems, it does not blink. In these utterly arresting poems, Derrick Harriell gives us a life's scope: tenderness and violence, memory and its force on the present, fatherhood, fertility, the work of being both a parent and a parent's grown son. *Come Kingdom* is a singular work of craft, vision, and empathy." —CATHERINE PIERCE

"In *Come Kingdom*, Derrick Harriell constructs a pulsating and provocative world of flesh, memory, and fantasy, where the celestial and the purgatorial come face to face. We readers witness this moving and jarring encounter, at turns terrifying and tender. The book culminates in two exuberant works, an elegiac crown of sonnets and a spectacular reinvocation of the many figures who appear through-out the collection. If poetry is memory and memory is a kind of afterlife, then *Come Kingdom* is Harriell revealing to us the many spirits his one gorgeous, lyric world can hold." —PATRICK ROSAL

"*Come Kingdom* by Derrick Harriell is a continuous motion of intense poems that are often hypnotic mic-drop moments driven by lyric and the precision of the line/stanza. Call *Come Kingdom* a def execution of language. I call *Come Kingdom* a mind-blowing experience—a tender reflection of one poet's life laid bare in the public sphere. I will not forget these poetic compositions (jewels) from a poet who leaves nothing on the metaphorical mat. I don't know whether to cry, clap, laugh, slap, or hug somebody—maybe I'll do them all. *Come Kingdom* is unafraid to operate in those complicated spaces, that once investigated, makes us our whole selves." —RANDALL HORTON

"Derrick Harriell's brilliant *Come Kingdom* pounds like a jackhammer. He explores the landscapes of masculinity, family, and responsibility, and illuminates his own unique path through language, where joy and grief sing the same song. Rich, dynamic, full of invention and wordplay, Harriell's poetry documents those king-doms we are given, and the kingdoms we create." —JANUARY GILL O'NEIL

Come
KINGDOM

SOUTHERN MESSENGER POETS

Dave Smith, *Series Editor*

DERRICK HARRIELL

Come

KINGDOM

POEMS

LOUISIANA STATE UNIVERSITY PRESS | BATON ROUGE

Published by Louisiana State University Press
lsupress.org

LSU PRESS PAPERBACK ORIGINAL

DESIGNER: Mandy McDonald Scallan
TYPEFACE: Livory

Thanks to the Academy of American Poets, *Birmingham Poetry Review*, *The Langston
Hughes Review*, *Literary Matters*, *Mississippi Review*, and A Poetry Congeries for being a
home to these poems.

Library of Congress Cataloging-in-Publication Data
Names: Harriell, Derrick, author.
Title: Come kingdom : poems / Derrick Harriell ; Dave Smith, series editor.
Description: Baton Rouge : Louisiana State University Press, [2022] |
    Series: Southern messenger poets
Identifiers: LCCN 2021059802 (print) | LCCN 2021059803 (ebook) | ISBN
    978-0-8071-7797-6 (paperback) | ISBN 978-0-8071-7823-2 (pdf) | ISBN
    978-0-8071-7824-9 (epub)
Subjects: LCGFT: Poetry.
Classification: LCC PS3608.A78138 C66 2022 (print) | LCC PS3608.A78138
    (ebook) | DDC 811/.6—dc23
LC record available at https://lccn.loc.gov/2021059802
LC ebook record available at https://lccn.loc.gov/2021059803

for my parents
Cassandra McKinley
and Floyd Harriell
Thank you for life

CONTENTS

Come

KINGDOM

COME

we're losing her / come see her
come leave us / she has your face
or your mother's mother's / can't you see
her in these hands / this bleeding-
tissue-sized blanket in my cup / looking perfect
funneling down some mortuary-
commode / remember we told
our mothers don't believe in morgues
or gynecologists' come
concepts / remember a vicious half-
decade of family planning / you believing
practice was better than bearing / that all
we needed was strong water and
a stronger push / we have all this
restroom procession / who says
she shouldn't have some name / room where
baby scent splatters like ravaged
contents of come carry / you had me at
baby / the moment this train
kept aborting / keep the engine
coming / she decided two months
was enough hellos to become
a martyr / promise you'll mention her
between breaths of keep
trying / that after we make love
you'll keep fathering / remember
all the fathers you could've been /
your come-stricken resembling
crowns of keep miscarrying

HOMECOMING KING

my mother suffers
from fibromyalgia and can only
listen to Gladys Knight
during the day / each night
she's a prisoner
to the revolver my father
placed to her head
a million bruises ago / each night
she counts threats
like sheep / says trauma
is a son-of-a-bitch /
tricky little fucker who shadows
like the man / Jeff / who came after
my father split / I still
think of killing Jeff / I'm unsure
that not doing so makes me
a conservationist / I believe
he should be honored /
I've only thought of killing once /
of all the shitty people I've met
it's like winning the fucking lottery /

I'm going somewhere with this /

four months ago my father left
the jailhouse / I'm told he spent
a month in solitary confinement
for fighting with himself / he swears
it was some boogeyman
with tattoos and red hair
a mile-long rap sheet /
three months ago
I wired my father get-by-money
from a Walmart in Mississippi /
two months ago

no one could find my father /
two days ago my father called
and no one could find me / yesterday
my sister said she gave him get-by-money /

I haven't seen my uncles
since being racist became cool again /
I wonder which taverns
they're haunting / I wonder
the phantasm haunting them /
one of my uncles donates plasma
for twenty dollars a pop /
hasn't worked a job
since his old lady stabbed him
in the forearm / this was before
my grandma died
and everything around us
started getting old /
even newborn babies
started getting old /

my father wants to know
if we've made our son a sibling
to help bury us / says
it's my birthright to be carried
by a daughter's hands / sometimes
I call my sister and hang up
before she answers / I call
my mother and hang up before
she begins mentioning death

AT THE UROLOGIST'S

last week my uncle had a heart attack and died
on the floor of his one-bedroom apartment /
his body discovered on Wednesday /
we don't know how long he'd been lying there /
last week a friend lost half her nose /
face cancer removal / I'm sitting in a urologist's
waiting room trying to retrace the nose
I remember / I'm sitting in a urologist's waiting room
waiting to die from too much waiting /
I'm at this waiting stage of my life
and I don't know when things became this way /
two elderly women walk across the room
holding hands / they collectively do paperwork /
one calls the other mom / I'm considering
every bad decision / I'm considering the condition
of the testicles I'm sitting on / I'm considering
the health of sperm and blood and urine /
the price of these things inside me / what Dear Lord
are they really for / a middle-aged man
in a cowboy hat leans against the front desk
clutching a yellow paper / he's whispering
to the secretary / he's asking why our Maker
manufactures all this complicated beauty

HOW TO EFFECTIVELY PROVIDE
A SEMEN SAMPLE

they'll tell you wait three days
then make a wish
in a tiny specimen cup /
tell you shit
about healthy and unhealthy sperm
about how many millions are required /
you'll do what you're told
because these days you don desperation
like a robe / these days you carry a child
in your throat and a fistful of seeds
in your abdomen / you'll wait three days
ignore the breeze across your lap when
your favorite Memphis weather girl declares
today there's sun / they'll tell you dangers
of contamination / how you'll repeat the process
until it's done / you'll have a half-hour
to transport the sample from your home
bathroom to the hospital lab / there a shaman
smiles a funeral through you / you'll wonder
if she knows about the weapon
in your coat pocket / you'll wonder
if she knows you're carrying a million
darlings in your tiny cup

HUNGER

a tarantula can survive
more than two years without
eating / yesterday I ate
a cheeseburger large enough
to feed a continent
of tarantulas / last week
a rusted truck hung itself
in an abandoned field /
fifty thousand spiders
might inhabit an acre
of open field / the South is full
of open fields / my mouth is full
of spiders /

my urologist prefers to rest
his hand on my leg when
discussing lab results / his face
studies numbers and percentages /
he says something about bad
and worse / something about
low motility / I say something
about nests or heritage /
something about magnolias
stringing me starved /

I remember believing
I would die hungry / a bully
punched me in the stomach
while everyone chewed / I remember
a punch was enough to change
the blood in my gut / a smack
enough to turn my Black into
a barely damaged branch /

he says low motility or
surgery / I drive home with a tarantula
inching down my throat / don't you
remember moths don't have stomachs /
remember my belly howling when
my liver became an axe

CLOMIPHENE

my urologist says he's unsure
when asked about side effects / says men
haven't been test-monkeyed
long enough to know / says everything
has a side effect / everything
is a side effect / the woman of your dreams
has a side effect / oligoasthenoteratozoospermia
is a side effect / when I was fifteen
I rubbed Retin-A on my face
for a whole summer / ran to the mirror
each morning for evidence
of disappearing acne / the next summer
my mother warned me
of having babies before I was old enough
to buy tequila / said a baby could ruin things /
said a life of blue and solitude
is a side effect / when I was fifteen
I carried golf bags for rich white men / I remember
a brutal summer / I remember my Retin-A-
residue-face burned holes
through a season / I've been told
God created most things before creating
us / that maybe we weren't created
at all / that humans are merely a side effect
of rain and wildflower / that at the root
I'd accept a seared face
if it meant she'll believe in fantasies
like her mother / how each night her mother
places a pill in my hand and releases
a bouquet of faith / how each night we dream
of footsteps / like Galway's poem / we dream
of footsteps after making love
and all the promised side effects
of matrimony

THE IN VITRO MYTH

I know a man who'll commit murder
for fifteen thousand dollars / he'll wait
in shadows / approach a stranger
cock the hammer and release
a pot of gold in your dreamy head /
once I was watching Locked Up Abroad /
Zoe was captured in an Ecuadorian airport
wearing six kilos of heroin / she'd spend
eight years in an Ecuadorian underworld /
she'd perish on her back with a shank
in her side and a wish on her mouth /
she'd never get fifteen thousand dollars
because the dope never landed in London /

I tell my urologist all this
when he whispers the price of in vitro /
tell him my parents once divorced
over fifteen thousand dollars and a bad
addiction / tell him my father once drove
a fifteen-thousand-dollar car into a decade
of ache / say how worthless I feel each time I pray
a Kardashian loses its wings /

once a wealthy friend took me to a South Beach
strip club / we drank champagne
and rained bills on a runway of want / piloted
our table until the moon waned / until
Angel recovered the last wish / watched it cloud
around like a field of dandelion seeds
on a parachute / maybe fifteen thousand
wishes landing into the holy well

I HATE MY FATHER FOR HIS VASECTOMY

each day my aunts call asking what I plan to do /
telling me you've finally hit rock bottom
saying moss is growing all around you /
I tell them I plan to do nothing / I've tried
saving you my whole life / back when
you crashed your Harley and seemingly
broke every small god from the waist down
I fed you Crown while we loathed
in a river of Muddy Waters / you swore
Muddy was an all of the above answer
for any question darkness could present /
my mother swore wiping your ass was harder
than taking you back each time you went absent /
you healed as all good boogeymen do /
wiped blues from your face
then continued your quest of overthrowing
kingdoms / I've seen whole husbands
turn half-king around you / seen you
move into another man's castle after
hauling his things to the sad side of town /
I always thought a love triangle would finish you /

my aunts hate me when I tell them
I plan to do nothing / they don't say it
but I've been hated enough times to know /
I'm told hate is like holding your breath
and expecting someone else to suffocate / sometimes
I hold my breath until I'm almost blue /
I hold my breath until my phone rings
and someone tells me you're suffocating
and everything around you is deep blue /

you called three days ago /
we shared our favorite scars and laughed
at my aunts for thinking you couldn't be saved
by godsend greater than me / you said
you'll die in the rapture of a speakeasy's last call /
I told you I was coming home in two weeks /
you told me the sky is falling on its face

OPTOMETRIST

if seeing was a sense I valued then
this morning I'd be on my way to see
an optometrist / instead I'm watching
the way shadows crowd outside my dining room
window / I've released the blinds
outside Mississippi is a bloody blur /
clouds gather to hold court / deliberate
the worth of our sun / today is confederate
gray / if I'm going blind I wonder
if I've seen enough / for every compelling
Mt. Hood kingdom-ornament outside
Portland hotel windows I've squinted
at the sight of an outlook burned grim / voyeur
of rude suffering when viewing
my granddaddy's blind resolve crumble
like a burning watchtower / he says he doesn't mind
not seeing because my grandma's face fills
the void / I too only see her in darkness /
only see another kind of kingdom
with my eyes shut / this morning my child
burrowed inside my chest and became
another heart / his breathing printed an album as
I blindly studied the darkroom

RESURRECTIONS

for a while I'd learned
to go without / annual checkups
and hands that examine my mouth /
life is like that when your insurance
is on the mend / when you send
your final twenty to the feet
of some stranger named Candy /
too much candy the dentist says
after my long hiatus / *too much candy*
and coffee and red wine / I'd known
of things that stain / how impossible
scrubbing blood from a basement floor
can be / *how come you waited so long* /
don't you know they could've all been dead by now
he asks / but I don't speak with a mouth full of glut /
don't speak fearing a congregation of tears
might rouse / he's drilling like there's treasure
in my mouth / like my head's a marooned kingdom
worth mining until all the castles are recovered

WHITE KNIGHT

she places his small body on a scale /
we watch the numbers climb / he hasn't been running
a fever lately / he's been singing a kingbird's
song / she sings a kingbird's song when examining
his ears / totes instruments like swords and spears / says
we really want to get him near the fiftieth percentile /
the tension is a fever / a consumed Percocet / my child
a patient with no country / I'm breaking like a country
with no capital / if percentile felt like love
we'd tell our children I percentile you before leaving /
if the word spectrum sounded like tenderness
we'd greet our wives with bouquets of spectrum /
I'm saying I can't remember my pediatrician
through all this white / can't remember if
she rode in on a horse / my child's pediatrician holds
his hand while brandishing a needle
like a dagger / she swears it'll only hurt for half a windfall

BENIGN OCCIPITAL EPILEPSY

is violent twitching / unbridled snitching
electrical / is oxcarbazepine / milliliters / is
milligrams / hightailing highway 55 jaundiced
girding your sphincter / is Memphis / is
Le Bonheur / COVID pacing takeoff / is
purple / gray / debased bubble / is
authorization shaking emergency stamping
neurologists / is psychologists / insurances / ID
graveyards no plot to piss / is waterless / is
not needleless / but bandages / and
neurologists / internships / Dr. Green
heaving / hemorrhage / is electro-
encephalograms like cavernous / is
ransoms / bedside diagnosis / penniless
I won't let nothing happen to you
father shit / is shaking / quaking / 50
pound gloat palpitating / father pound
phantom pulsating / debating / decisions /
precision / grinding a ledge's beckon / is
jump / like catch / like bitch / like come
quick / never saw that ditch / like
fall / like small things with huge
talls / like shake / pulling breathe
lever too late / mates yelling shit like *that's
yo mama's traits* / is wait / clinical / not
not minimal / but not not chemical / general
lovers splitting because visceral / is
triggering in your quivering / that
splintering / benign Valtoco / junkie
snorted miracle

WILD HORSES

pretend you don't know me when dragging my body
down a bleeding highway and I'll pretend
to do the same / if it's friendly fire then you probably
had it coming / probably burned some kingdoms
when no one was watching but I don't care much /
gives none fucks like pigeons after brunch / I've told you
migrate this world and conquer all desirable
provinces / I'll do the same / like this woman who knows
your body better than me / who affirms *he's most likely*
the problem / like a body and a problem can share
a province / like a problem and a body can share
street corners / remember my cousin's gun jammed under
a streetlight's apathy / we paraded abroad and I believe
this the first time it's been mentioned / four boys made out
with the afterglow on a midnight's porch / how forgetful
an almost death is / we don't mention your gynecologist
like the adolescent daughter my uncle never mentions / sometimes
I pimp past aborted bluebirds because an ex is holding
my concentration / your gynecologist thinks of you when
dragging her husband down highways of crumble / don't you
feel it in your stomach like a fetus catching the holy ghost

UNDERGROUND KING

for Ermias Asghedom (Nipsey Hussle)

do you know what it is to make a wish knowing
it's a waste since before you even made it /
there was a guy back home who sold roses
out his trunk / he'd wait outside clubs
and ask if anyone wanted to buy a pretty lady
a keepsake / something to ensure
she remembers you / something sweet
to accompany the drinks you'd gifted
all night / I remember watching gangsters
buy roses like lottery tickets / chase women
all the way to their cars / remind them
which drink came from which pocket /
plead to be remembered /

do you know badgers make their homes
underground / while we celebrate the day
they wait around for dark / all the men I love
are nocturnal / stumbling vampires
in search of midnight roses / one night I stumbled
out a juke and couldn't find my car /
haunted neighborhood blocks for what seemed
like leap years / I swear my beard grew white
that night / started tracking my own footprints
in snow / do you know what it is to track
oneself / it requires divine patience / just when
you think you've found your target
it moves / the way a sober shadow might /
the way an almost granted wish does / the way
a badger moves once the last person on earth
places her head to the pillow / it peeks
above ground to let the bobcats know
it isn't dead

QUARANTINED

after Mark Doty

if there were sirens for this
they'd be sirening / if
this was post-apocalyptic drama
then fiends would be
fiending / let's say
I'm the villain in theater
of no-touching / no-touching
savior of relentless no-
script / hero of saving no-
thing / a crackhead predicted
this / said *there shall be*
the year of no-touching /
the world will know
what it is to kiss
distancing / remember
believing in nothing when
Ezekiel sirened *little buddy*
don't you believe the King's
coming back like baby daddies
and tax returns / remember
what you know good
Hollywood / crackheads saving
more lives than Black Jesus /
Jesus is real / I've seen him
in quarantine / invisible miracle-
giver / remember a child's seizure
swarming like a crown of thorns /
the Messiah's body becoming
bread and grape-fiend tableau / remember
lonely hands / an errand / D-Nice
D-jaying / miscarriages gathering /
records never supposed to scratch

40 DAYS AND 40 NIGHTS

rooted in the haven you made home /
sinful floorboards / pregnancy catastrophes
and all / mold collecting throughout gutters /
vultures pitch tents and after thirteen days
the grizzlies can sniff the determination /
she says *granny said a man and woman*
wanting to make a baby should keep on
keeping on until someone starts
dreaming of whales / somewhere Moby Dick
is dreaming a school of prey
he'll devour / somewhere a Black body
is molested in sirens / somewhere
a twelve is reaching for a holster under a God
who can't believe this shit is happening
again / God is mumbling something
about free will / ancestors are screaming
something about stewardship / the woman
in lockdown is pleading something
about an unblessed union / she's saying
honey pray with me before
we make love / *dear Lord* / *please*
bless us with life / *we're good people*
who don't ask for much / *please*
bless my husband's body with perfection
and our coming together with precision /
if it is your will dear Lord
we'll keep doing this because
what else is there to do / *everyone outside*
is dying / *just yesterday a boy outside*
our window wouldn't stop running /
just yesterday my husband came
to me with barren eyes
and wouldn't stop coming

IMMACULATE CONTRACEPTION

after Nas's "Rewind"

the shot came back
into his body behind
permanent dam /
his hands unclenched
her neck / she breathed
inside it keep / he
hummed *tonight girl*
a making we're think /
the neighbor's terrier
trotted backwards into
the crib next door / a bark
reentered its teeth
like choke / those lovers
spat bubbly back into
secondhand flutes / smiled
with open vows / said
you see to good / he
closed the door of his coupe /
drove home without using
the rearview / Stevie Wonder
blared throughout the bathroom /
shaving cream was removed
from his cheeks while Stevie blew
lovely she isn't / a band
backslid like believers
moving further from
lover's leap

TALKING DIRTY TO THE KINGDOM

after Yusef Komunyakaa

I.

the pornography gods are punishing
theatergoers this afternoon / a Manhattan
socialite garnishes her nose in a bloody noose /
everyone's begging for a body beneath

Brooklyn billboard altars / children play dead
on decaying playgrounds throughout
the backbone of this kingdom / these
are the sacred moments / permanent photos

of loathe / the sun has a curious way of not
renouncing / a cop murders a Black boy and pigeons
predict darkness for a decade / a Bronx vagabond
says nothing for a year straight / a surgeon

dirty talks a blade handle / a lonely adolescent disrobes
in the fever of a stranger's suffering / the world
is impotent / Isis is breaching and all around pyramids
grow from the ground like eager baby-makers

II.

I'm having dinner with a liberal who hugs trees
and little Black boys she'll never meet / she says
Mother Nature is barren and human beings
the Lord's boner / says the highest gods roam

the lowest heavens / *did you know there are kingdoms*
beneath our feet / spectacular winged things
guarding thrones and queens / she says this then
finishes a glass of Caymus / says this then tells

of raging fires on faraway continents / the food
between us is a landfill of once roaming / her mallard
dinner an unknown offering of once flying / I've heard
purgatory is right here on earth / right here in this

establishment / here / in the spaces between her cutlery
and my mourning / earlier today somebody back home
became an adolescent ancestor / I want to share
this / want to know more about her lower heavens

III.

there's a time and place for kicking the bucket
says the bullet to the body / says
the plastic surgeon's blade to the housewife
before trimming her centerfold recovery / says

restored housewife to the husband sending
her burning to a gynecologist / yes Lord
such beautiful offerings for the ugly / unnecessary
endings / we go even when we don't have to /

restored housewife will soon become reality TV
martyr / faith moves her to testify / she
fashions a ruptured disaster for the camera / hopeless
skin frowns like Chicagoans in December / yesterday

a cockroach braced as my shoe raged down
like a coffin penetrating the ground / yesterday
I shaved gray from my face and felt pretty / yesterday
I fell from a bucket and landed in a tomb of wine

IV.

someone needs to do something about Kanye /
or maybe / Kanye needs to do something about
someone / or possibly / if your name begins with a
K you shouldn't be allowed to marry someone

whose name begins with a K / or perhaps / you two
shouldn't be allowed to have a baby whose name
begins with a K / I'm saying three Ks in one frame
is an alarming gospel / or maybe

the crosses failed me because I couldn't hang /
can we be failed by artistry stranger than
a hummingbird in a dope house / or a dope-
fiend catching the holy ghost in the middle of a dope

cathedral / Kanye is spreading his god's word
like the drunkard outside the McDonald's on Wabash
who told me Jesus still walks Chicago like sanctified
peasants parading Michelangelo's pearly paradise

V.

you only like white-looking Black
girls she stated / the way a statement
and beg can hold each other
the way we'd just finished holding in the

humiliation of my parent's basement /
it's cold down there in November
and space heaters don't do shit
when accusatory palms turn calamity

frostbit / enough to make you question
your keepers / question the maps on
your palms and whether there's actual royalty
in those tracks / *touch me like you*

touch them redbones she called for /
like she'd known about the first time I'd seen
Apollonia topless in *Purple Rain* / she'd known
how my slight body was flooded in praise

VI.

Whitney I'm praising you from a porch swing
in Mississippi / been wanting to tell you how
I was saving my virginity and all the mystery
of my twelve-year-old body for you / saving

my maiden orgasm for you / wanting to save you
Rachel Marron as only a puberty-packing Black
boy could / how dare he so begrudgingly become
your bodyguard / how dare Farmer act like that shit

was uneventful / Whitney I couldn't throw a knife
into the rib of an oak but swear I would've protected you
from that creepy-ass dude / at twelve I could outrun
the neighborhood and would've taken

that bullet too / our production would've ended
this way / you running from the plane to me / zebra
royal headdress a halo / me not letting go / sanctified /
becoming more man each moment / head buried in you

VII.

of course Willie Dee would defile the throne
not knowing any better / and of course
a blue-haired blonde-eyed virgin
would save our dear warrior goddess

from savages looking to ravage
her body / savage feelers craving Black
fruit has always been a pastime of
the barbaric / the kind that leaves kingdoms

in smithereens / but Zula was an uncommon kind
of country / bombastic island of horsepower
and Grace / didn't you see that stallion
galloping like a reverie in odyssey / toting the Lord's

bless-weapon staff / boomeranging back like
a Cadillac / panty-less in holy-lit establishment / alluring
sorceress that even old Willie thirsted
to taste her runway's underbelly

VIII.

you spirited trauma religiously / your father
who forsook you like roadkill morphed
into concrete bars of verses that raptured me /
keepers who abandon the loudest eventually

suffer in quiet / that's on everything / come
with me / don't you know we can still be
GOAT of something / right now in barbershops
throughout hoods your voice is fisting a church

of devotion / right now in Chicago and Atlanta
and New Orleans and Houston and Philly
and Milwaukee and Oakland someone is being
crowned you resurrected / Damn Pac

we still haven't moved the homeless into
the White House / Black men are still disappearing /
if I go missing I implore this world of mine to burn
everything everywhere until everyone comes home

IX.

Artemis has ushered in her favorite wild things /
sister-of-the-bride untamed temptress in
mouth-watering bed-hole / when a woman's
getting married in the projects you must bare

all the peepholes / there has to be snake holes
slithering underworld of gluttonous yum /
hallelujah / a woman's getting hitched
this afternoon / in-laws getting stoned

in greenrooms / outside the courtyard sweltering
chapel / Miss Shirley / glaucoma clergy
Chimera / I'm a chitterling benediction from
beholding my auntie unveiled / from twisting

a knob I couldn't untwist / consumed nude
sunken breasts / a rendezvous / auntie
Artemis / ambushed bone / ring bearer peeper /
godhead erected / ghetto Alpheus

X.

we promise we're only staying for one dirty
martini / enough time for us both to fall
in love / enough time for us to buy a young woman
a shot / to put something on her rent / whatever

keeps her snaking this pole / like some pole charmer
some snake charmer the way I'm bewitched in
the endlessness of patent leather heels / I knew
this was bad when admission was free / this

was bad when the bartender called it happy hour /
we're taught to never leave anything free
behind / to drink the free of buy one get one /
you saunter from the ATM like a Jinn / this woman

surrounds us like a gallery / we're the only ones
alive right now / the vibrant purple smoke a ghost
of newborn / she's climbing towards a pink
ceiling / we heave offerings before falling invisible

XI.

Black men kneel and the emperor
isn't wearing any clothes / small town mas and pas
throw bigotry against the rancor side
of a pickup / one red summer I fell in love

with a redhead in a pickup who votes
republican / she was highway heat melting
in Mississippi like the daughter of Hades /
lost at a light we located the bridge between

political and pivotal / if you've never made love
to a republican in Mississippi then you ain't done
nothing / you ain't learned to walk with a cotton field
in your throat and a magnolia in your head /

you might find yourself debating prochoice over
corn whiskey after making love / might find her
taking off religion right in front of you / removing
bloodlines / kneeling / like she has something to say

XII.

the freak show gods are freaking essential
workers this evening / a mother ruins emergency
mold and deems it blessed loaf / infirmary exiles
moan beneath East Side spirituals / housewives

rise from excavated crack vials / ta-da / unmasked
stickup moms rob at dumb-point / viruses spread
like proposals in strip-joints / dear constituency /
have a vaccine for me / a dictator's fuckery / dynasty

on child support / this the desperate juncture / release
the captives / we have the ransom / we have
the lovers / videophone distanced / indecency
angled / peer-to-peer coming / bitcoins in

breach-mode / OnlyFans in freak-mode / Tweets in
cheat-code / DM me / we could use some company /
you show yours and I'll show mine / speak
dirty / nasty / all these freak-cures have mercy

MANDRAKE BOUQUET

the starving liturgy is here / my seething
adolescent feet ailing / hands
sand-raked blistered / ears ringing
racism's hammer / me in all my
juvenility / Adidas donning
mule / Friday doused / hotbox juked / feast
fire-lit / Sandra's wand striking / christening
gifts / voilà / we're wading in Chi-Lites and

singe / basking / in fry-lights and
binge / chef's birthing a sumptuous bird / trap-
house turned church / nourishment crisp
keeping a shindig in peace / *Father thank you
for this evening* / heathens worship hands
like gristle in graves of grease

even heathens worshipped his fingers
that rang through ringside weekends /
Sandra's lipstick heartbeat red / father's boots
David Ruffin rematch ready / Friday
night fights / mother haymaking
divorce threats because his collar
been beating a plum-punch / everyone knows
she don't fuck with plum and won't

eat them neither / Friday night's making up /
white-toweled making out / alimony canvas
recount / my refereeing / split rekindling
won't stop bleeding / lovecard scored / undefeated
broken-hearted draw / breathe /
no one sorry about anything

no one sorry about anything / dear
sister / don't be sorry about the countries
you dreamed furnished in unicorns
and mermaids / your monsters always had
the most dangerous beauty / your dreams
the most beautiful consequences / you knew
what it meant to risk bus-ride ridicule in the name
of future rainbows / what it meant to be

a vibrant skyline in a room of streetlights / and
I won't apologize for dreaming your birthdays
away / deflowered guidance undone / see
I've been tied to my own dreams / been chasing
an ordinary horse / teach me to ride things that fly /
I'll submit to the sky in your name

I'll submit to the sky in your name mother /
submit to religion in your name / I know you're
Allah's daughter / Nation daughter / Brady X's
daughter / seen pictures / little girl you in all white /
headpiece all white / granddaddy's heart and bowtie
all black / today mother / there won't be any pork
falling from our forks / no remorse from our
foreclosures / I'm here to admit we're our

dancing more than our slips / you rocking
my being sober / forgive me when only testifying
tragedies / I've been a glutton for alleyway
robberies / remembering an adulterated youth over
heavy pours / nowadays I've been remembering new
yesterdays that shake me out the blue

yesterdays shake me out the blue
like somersaulting sharks in Atlantic
waters / the waters are fine mother
get in / bring your mother too / how about
we launch a parade in heaven's waters
mother / ask grandma are there waterslides
where she resides / what they call the waves
surrounding them /

heaven sounds too shallow a body
to harbor Lucille / too definitive
a destination for someone who preferred
the land / I dream grandma still building
gardens of eating in the afterlife / her feathers
tranquil as a whole heaven of herons

tranquil as a whole heaven of herons
hatching an overcast of flight / don't you
remember grandma perched
in her rocking chair while children
lost their minds around her the way
children lose their minds when
growing wings / when believing in free-
willing to war with whomever blocks

the saving of the girl next door / it's always
a good time for fights that redden the face
of even the blackest cat / grandmaster grandma
would sit pawns on her lap / say *next time*
baby move two spaces / push that rook in
a corner / never let them see you cower

we made sure they never saw us cower
honored our uncles pretending to be
them / *I'll be Carl and you be Kenny* /
they demanded we be another thing /
you be lawyer and you be Wall Street /
how not to own the blackhearts our
chessboards forced down our mouths
like knights of white / to stay clever

when the game gambits in checkmate
communities / stay player when the game karens
in gated communities / tonight I'm calling
each / one by one / that's six phone calls /
six whole testimonies / six ways of praising twelve
hands that blocked caskets whenever they came calling

hands that blocked caskets whenever they came calling /
voice that whispered *leave the corner before*
they start dumping / oh my / you've always been
there / and I've always been pretentious / what made me
believe there was some intuition spelling me *bend*
the corner right before a bullet seared
the ghost of our SUV / made me believe
chance corrected the semi just before

it forced us off the road / I swear we were two
eye blinks from becoming the guest of honor in a sad
Ellis Wilson painting / instead I'll dance like a saint
on a T-shirt / dance because that's an everlasting
sacrament / please don't silence the gratitude / holler
until every utterance sounds like amen

until every word sounds like amen /
until mornings are born-again forests of faith /
until losses become blistering lessons of praise /
until the ground flowers merry-go-rounds of rejoice /
until embracing wonder becomes choice / until
my voice is rubble and remnants and charred
and my chords are rusted from throating /
I'll keep having too many mandrakes

wrapped around me like a murder
of mothers harvesting the afterworld / dear world
I'm an undeserving baby-daddy hoping to live
long enough to hand-deliver my pension
to my son / dear son / you were Mississippi-stork
delivered / wrapped fiercely / like above-ground mummies

we wrapped you fiercely like below-ground breath /
in a suffocating hospital room you announced life
by keeping one hand in the after / and there we were /
small country of bleak and bereft / of baby and blue
weighing down our faith the way hospital floors
can bury family-tree fruit / the way some trees
can't survive a tornado's angry / the way
mothers become tornados when newborns

won't breathe / why wouldn't you breathe son /
we arranged a nursery and funeral / had I recorded
your coming to life I'd play the revelation loud
enough to remove any doubt of how much you were
needed / because you exhumed / the way all prophets do /
half dead / half pulling eyes from our heads

half dead / half pulling eyes from our heads /
half on time / half late again / damn near
half the tardy marks on your report card
are mine / blame your mother for the other
half / lately mornings been half
a casualty / find us driving with half
a mourning melting from the face of half
our windshield / even a car feels half-

collisions / *look at all those kingdoms dad*
you say each morning we past Kingdom
Cemetery in Oxford, Mississippi / *dad*
can they have so many kingdoms in one place /
I never tell those headstones aren't citadels /
hallways of half dust / a half-man's half hallelujah

hallways of half dust / a boy's half hallelujah
howls from the other room / we are quarantined
half nothings splitting despair like a pair of
coyotes counting tracks in ruins / nothing can
ruin us / we've known this since the beginning
of our bitterness / since you claimed
you could eat me and I wouldn't know
I was dust / wouldn't know I'm only

something worth seeing when filtered
through you / *you know if I die first*
I'll haunt you you say / I know this how
I knew granddaddy wouldn't see the vaccine
Promised Land / coyote me dear / watch how
babies and blessings start to fall from our beards

babies and blessings start to fall from our beards
before we order appetizers / oh this French Quarter
hums on quarantine eve / this spectacle
of desperate is everything I've wanted to sink
my dreams into / the streets are teeming with
saints and children prepared to save
some kingdoms from sinners / from us
zombies hoping to sling some nightmares

for one last nasty go at it / right mother / we've
never appeared more enchanting / more
together than in the bull's-eye of this French
bistro / merlot lags down your blouse mother /
the only thing more saved than us / bring the
quarantines / we have nothing to need these nights

we have nothing to need these nights /
in the a.m. no caffeine can get us right /
just yesterday I swallowed a whole
embryo of sorrow / gave birth
to a broken adieu / mother
I watched you board your flight
from a mangled wing
of yesterday / you boarded

and like the last umpteen years
I only imagined holding your
wings / only cowards apologize
on paper / you taught me to accept both
flowers and fists like a man / here I am
bracing my face for forgiveness

brace your face for forgiveness pops
I'm on one and it's the fuck it hour / done
hoodooed your being so often
it's a record I play better than *Voodoo* / done
placed your Stetsons in a fire and watched
a repenting boogeyman / done conceded
this Marvin way isn't for me / I've stuffed
my body with damage and hooch

to feel what you feel / leaned into an after-
bar looking for Satan and a woman to smash
my virtue / remember the summer we watched
the sunrise like a lotus until our mouths burgeoned
bourbon / remember you slurring how beautiful
I was / remember seething with starve all season

ANNO DOMINI

(the father to the son)

you came and everything turned like mud dust fingering
sanctity / it pulsed like temples when shelters go empty / you
were born and everything in that hospital was Hail Mary
vulnerability / your blue pulled out my ex-wife's bemoaning like
holy motherfucker / like a preemie heaving to strangle my legacy

(the father to the son)

you were born with an umbilical cord
lynching you to your mother's core /
the bluest thing assembled / almost dead
little blue thing me and your mother
put together / the hospital cheered you
little Rocky eating Clubber Lang's fists /
Saint Joseph's baby southpaw too stubborn
to die that February / so you lived
and we can talk / here we are / everything
had to be the way it went
for us to be here /

the first time I saved your life
I was just old enough to drive / pulled you
from the tub after you swallowed
murderous amounts of bathwater / your mother
dropped you in and split / didn't say shit /
just walked away / if not for me you
would've left this life abruptly / I pulled you
from that water and you were more blue
than Miles Davis's crew / more dead
than your grandfather the June
he passed and nobody knew / not even
the German Shepard could tell
he'd moved to the quieter side of hell /

last winter you heard I was homeless /
hated me for the home-going
you wouldn't afford / don't you feel holy
when praying I'll blow away / born-again

when discovering I'm merely man / your mother
and me etched vows in winter / made
snow-devils in your grandmother's garden /
you rolled about your mother's belly like
an almost ready snowball / an almost ripe
grenade awaiting detonation / an explosion
rumbling omen of break

(the father to the son)

sometimes you think
so much of yourself
don't you / you may
get that from me / just
like you get your wanting
to romance a bottle
of brown and take it
down like your favorite
stripper or bartender or
neighbor / don't you
feel it somewhere

quaking deep
beneath the mud
of what you pretend
to be / my son
we are one / don't
believe we're not /
I see through
the lightshow / through
the trophies you pose with
in pictures / I'm there
when you bury them
in ditches

(the father and the son sing to the holy kingdom)

this kingdom was always

dungeon of damnation

coaxing Black men

to trust a banged-up

American cut / maybe

there was a dream

glorious out there

for me / sanctuary

to make maimed

road beginnings

more than Alabamian

chanting haints / each time

my fantasy became

a runaway slave

misery showed ruthless

salutation / a darkness /

the Reaper I'm bound to

glory blessed in bruise

kingdom of not meant

nightmare of not shit

madman's chant of

paradise's virgins /

no matter what

the heavens will always be

more heavy

but repair

more perfectly when

the Supreme is in on

this thing / obscure like

me eating my heart out

at daybreak / just before

the season changes

all this ruin summons

my father's wraith

(the father to the son)

when the relapse comes
it doesn't ask
if it's an acceptable time /
neither does the goon
catching you slipping outside
your neighborhood bar /
he simply shows up and
demands what he wants /
and you / if you're not stupid /
empty your pockets
and sometimes the clothes
on your back / because
you know there are things
you can't control / you see
summer was good to me / then
that thing showed itself
out the shadows like the goon
I mentioned / that darkness
demanded everything / and I
surrendered because there's freedom
in victimhood / pleasure
in being something's slave

(the father to the son)

it strikes like a match / you
become a fire and every sin
you've swallowed or wrong
you've thrown into your past
lands on some hurt that leaves you
busted engine / the shakes
demonstrate how quickly
hooch can beat you basket-
case / nobody prepares you /
and when this lands / you won't
be released until it's satisfied
by the same ritual you freaked
when you begged it to find
refuge in you

(the son and the father sing to the holy kingdom)

dear kingdom /

won't you redeem

our hearts like

mended slums

after war-torn /

undo us pure

like unworn

flesh / bury

our abandoned /

our damned deities /

I'm a bastard

needing reparation /

needing fathers /

daughters to hold

my hand when

the Reaper's harvesting

my name from our land /

dear hornets' nest /

things that sting

hands that bleed like

abandoned heirs

desperate in wind /

dear regretful seeds

testaments of

deadbeat revival /

we'll come again

humming back

from netherworld

needing mothers /

sons to hold

our hands

during this exodus

when the cold pulls

life from our ground

KINGDOM COME

come name from land
     life from ground / come
         demon's rest

come kingdom

come melted matrimony
     dope-fiend refugees / come
         she

come kingdom

come relapse
     splendored starved / come
         chant

come kingdom

come below-ground feathers
     divine gospel of bird / come
         motherless

come kingdom

come Hail Mary headstone
     anthem's wound / come
         hooch

come kingdom

come sibling
     embryo dream / come
         zombies

come kingdom

come coyotes
       senile cemetery / come
              waiting room

come kingdom

come casket chorus
       pointers dumping / come
              coming

come kingdom

come rocking chairs /
       gardens of eating / come
              Allah

come kingdom

come mean
       miserable me / come
              free

come kingdom

come Chi-Lites / Temptations
       trap-house / come
              Stevie

come kingdom

come freak show
        annihilated audience / come
                red Mississippi

come kingdom

come mourning
        emergency anointed / come
                environmentalists

come kingdom

come gypsies
        conquered poles / come
                bread

come kingdom

come horsepower
        runway's sorceress / come
                underbelly

come kingdom

come Whitney and Vanity
        bodyguards and virginity / come
                Lake Minnetonka agony

come kingdom

come dope-fiend numb
        come-down crumbs / come
                priests

come kingdom

come plastic surgeons / rulers of
        scalpel and remake / come
            retake

come kingdom

come free will
        Hollywood pageantry / come
            plantation stank

come kingdom

come beasts
        badgers and bobcats / come
            aborted reapers

come kingdom

come possessed
        apathetic / come
            with no country

come kingdom

come mouths of split
        burning glut / come
            Candy

come kingdom

come cells
      scarecrow sand / come
            me

come kingdom

come aunties
      fields of in vitro / come
           clomiphene

come kingdom

come cemeteries
      semen / come
           beaming

come kingdom

come baby
      come come / come
           hug your brother

come kingdom

come mother
      come come this hurt is a murder / come
           come

ACKNOWLEDGMENTS

I want to thank my dear friend Dave Smith for selecting this book as part of LSU Press's Southern Messenger Poets series and everyone at the Press who had a hand in this collection. I want to thank my three readers: Drew Blanchard, Melissa Ginsburg, and Kiese Laymon. I want to thank every past, present, and future writer who has or will contribute to language and the production of art. I want to thank my family, friends, colleagues, and anyone who has extended love and light toward my kingdom. I want to thank Milwaukee for raising me and Mississippi for loving me. I want to thank the Mississippi Arts Commission for supporting this project and making space for us to create art. I want to extend my love and gratitude to Drake and April Harriell, my eternal tribe. And I finally want to send my soul to all the children I never had but in the words of Gwendolyn Brooks: "Believe me, I knew you, though faintly, and I loved, I loved you / All."